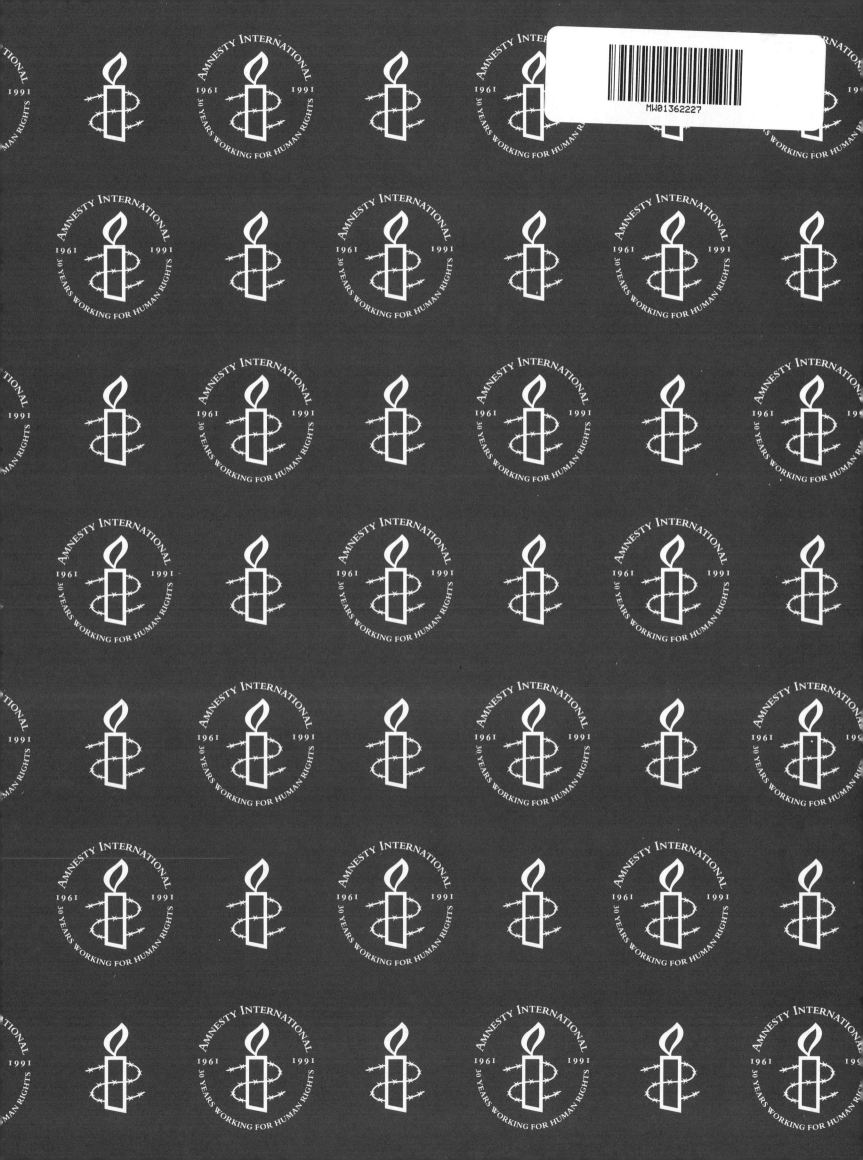

Thoughts on HUMAN DIGNITY and FREEDOM

Foreword by
ARTHUR MILLER

U N I V E R S E

ACKNOWLEDGMENTS

We wish to express our gratitude to Visions Photos, *Index on Censorship*, and the individual photographers, writers, and publishers, all of whom so generously contributed to this volume. Special thanks are due to Bob Cato and Ina Cooper, whose work on the Amnesty International calendar served as the inspiration for this book. In addition, we are indebted to Eric Baker, Susi Oberhelman, and Patrick Seymour at Eric Baker Design, Adele Ursone at Universe Books, Dorothy Caeser, Sherry Skibbe, and Helen Garrett, all of whom dedicated an enormous amount of energy and care in bringing this project to fruition in time for Amnesty International's thirtieth anniversary.

We mourn the passing of Hugh Swift (1943-1991), whose photograph of Nepal appears on pp. 58-59.

Published in the United States of America in 1991
by Universe
300 Park Avenue South, New York, NY 10010

©1991 Universe Publishing, Inc.

Printed in Singapore

Cover and Book Design: Eric Baker Design Associates, Inc.
Photo Editor: Ina Cooper
Front Cover Photo: *Kashi children, Xinjiang Province, China,* ©Ric Ergenbright
Back Cover Photo: *Soviet Armenia,* ©Dave Bartruff

All rights reserved. No part of this publication may be reproduced, stored in a retrieval system, or transmitted, in any form or by any means, electronic, mechanical, photocopying, recording, or otherwise, without prior permission of the publishers.

91 92 93 94 95 / 10 9 8 7 6 5 4 3 2 1

Thoughts on HUMAN DIGNITY and FREEDOM

FOREWORD

by
ARTHUR MILLER

IT IS BY NOW THE CONVENTIONAL WISDOM THAT everything is going from bad to worse these days. Perhaps so. But one thing has improved, it seems to me. People have a higher level of awareness than they used to where their rights as citizens and human beings are concerned. This is true not only here in the United States but, for example, in China and Europe and, yes, in the Soviet Union and the Eastern European countries. It doesn't mean that they can't be pushed around anymore but that they know very well when it is happening and that it cannot be acceded to as humanity's permanent fate.

The injection of human rights considerations into diplomacy, initiated in my country's case by the Carter administration, was regarded by many as an impractical and even ludicrous notion. But now, only a few years on, the mistreatment of a country's citizens by its government has a prominent place on the agenda of foreign relations nearly everywhere.

Amnesty International was not the first organization to emphasize the human rights infractions of national governments, but it has no doubt been most effective in one specific respect: it has applied the same standards to all countries regardless of their social and political systems. In the Western press and the common awareness this has not been the case until very recently. During the long years of cold war whole continents fell out of the Western consciousness as far as human rights were concerned. Latin America, Asia, Africa and even China were given very little notice by human rights advocates; it was as though their peoples, having no democratic history, didn't particularly mind being thrown into dungeons or executed for political dissent or merely for failure to salute with sufficient feeling.

We know now that the dream of freedom is universal, even if its meaning might differ from place to place. Certain fundamentals are the same everywhere—in no country are people indifferent to being tortured or jailed or mistreated for having dissident opinions. In no country is the appeal of freedom from fear of government a minor matter.

It may be that while we weren't looking society has evolved, progressed an inch or two. It doesn't mean that we won't blow up the planet or poison it unto death, merely that it is much harder than before to not know what we are doing. Amnesty, with its stream of documented reports from all over the world, is a daily, weekly, monthly assault on denial. For Amnesty the victims are no longer faceless, they have names and addresses and relatives and await the help of those who call themselves free. This volume is part of an immense record of Amnesty's work in keeping all of our heads above water. Anybody who wants to think of him or herself as a citizen of this world ought to know a lot about what is in it.

INTRODUCTION

THE LITTLE BOY WITH THE GOLDEN FACE TURNED SLOWLY IN HIS SLEEP. IN THE DIM GLOW OF THE NIGHT LAMPS, MEN, WOMEN, AND CHILDREN SPRAWLED AND CROUCHED IN THE SWAYING OF THE TRAIN. AMONG THEIR WRETCHED BUNDLES OF BLANKETS AND PANS, A SOLITARY FIGURE PICKED HIS WAY.

He found a space where the lamplight caught the features of the sleeping child. He thought to himself that if this dismal carriage, crammed with suffering humanity, were a garden, the gardeners would lift this fragile creature—like a beautiful new rose—out of the gnarled and crushed world around it. They would tend and foster it.

"This is a life of beautiful promise," he said to himself as he gazed upon the child. "This is a musician's face. This is the child Mozart. But there is no gardener for him. This little Mozart is condemned. It is the human race that is outraged here. What torments me is the sight of Mozart murdered."

The solitary figure rose and resumed his nocturnal journey through the corridors of the lumbering train. Perhaps none who saw him pass that night recognized him as the celebrated French aviator and author Antoine de Saint-Exupéry. War clouds were gathering. The carriages were filled with Polish workmen and their families forced across the continent in one of the great European migrations before World War II. But in the midst of that appalling turmoil, the sight of the sleeping boy, a golden fruit born of two peasants, was to stay forever in his memory—eventually to be transformed into the haunting figure of his legendary "Little Prince."

"What is essential," St.-Exupéry wrote, "is invisible to the eye." The invisible bonds that bind one human being to another. The invisible bonds of love. The inextinguishable idea of justice. Our ineluctable perceptions of the truth. The eternal qualities of courage, compassion, and honesty. The great potential in every human being. These are the invisible wellsprings of freedom and human dignity. But, like the delicate features of the sleeping child destined to be stamped with the agony of his generation, they have no gardener and no protector. Great minds, great ideas, great souls have faced a bitter fate. The record of history is replete with the stories of men and women who have paid with their lives for the courage of their convictions. Others have been silenced by interminable periods in prison. Some have "disappeared" without trace. Others have been hideously tortured and mutilated.

A few must stand as symbols for the rest. Aesop, the fifth-century Athenian who assembled the much-loved collection of animal fables, was thrown to his death from the Tarpeian Rock—accused of sacrilege. The aged Socrates, whose intellectual light has come to represent the birth of Western civilization, was sentenced to death by a vote of 280 to 220—accused of not believing in the gods of the state. St. Valentine, whose annual festival is an homage to love, was beheaded in A.D. 269—for marrying young lovers in defiance of an imperial ban. Francisco Ferrer, the genius of Spanish education, went before a firing squad in 1909 shouting "Long live the Modern School!" The prodigious Russian poet Osip Mandelstam, who defied Stalin, is rumored to have been last seen alive in a Siberian transit camp in the late 1930s reciting his own poetry to a circle of fellow prisoners.

It is sometimes mistakenly assumed that prisoners of conscience and victims of political or religious persecution are largely products of European cultures. Arabic society, Oriental history, biblical records, and African struggles have also been characterized by instances of individuals whose personal integrity or beliefs conflicted either with domestic or colonial rulers.

Reverberations of the French Revolution's cry of "Liberté, Fraternité, Egalité" reached the slaves of San Domingo in the Caribbean in 1791, at a time when this French colony served as the great slave market of the world. Out of its chaos rose François Dominique Toussaint L'Ouverture, himself a slave until the age of 45, who eventually succeeded—at least for a time—in thwarting the  imperial powers of France, Spain, and England. Following a bloody uprising, he abolished slavery and commanded that a constitution be written for free black men. A sample copy sent to Napoleon Bonaparte resulted in the dispatch of a punitive expedition to the colony which, using the time-honored treachery of a false offer of armistice, succeeded in capturing Toussaint L'Ouverture. He was shipped to Napoleon's dungeon in Fort de Joux, France, where he died in 1803, possibly the victim of deliberate starvation. Eight months later, the free state of Haiti was born—an ironic birthright for what has been at times one of the world's most dreaded police states.

In Africa, nationalists uphold the memory of leaders of anti-imperialist movements as diverse as 'Abd al-Kadir in Algeria, detained and exiled by the French in 1847, and Nicodemus, one of the Namibian leaders executed by German soldiers in 1904. More familiar is the South African chief, Albert Luthuli, winner of the 1961 Nobel Peace Prize. From 1945 until his death in 1967, Luthuli was a leading figure in the nonviolent opposition to apartheid in South Africa, active in a 1952 countrywide campaign against unjust laws, in which 8,500 men and women went voluntarily to prison, and four years later, one of 156 defendants in the famous Johannesburg treason trial (although massive public protests resulted in his subsequent release). In 1960, when Luthuli burned his passcard following the Sharpeville massacre, he was again sentenced to prison but, being too ill to serve his term, was fined instead.

The ferment aroused by the advent of Islam has been followed by centuries of philosophical and other differences among believers. The prophet Muhammad and his early followers faced ridicule, discrimination, and organized opposition. After years of denunciation, exile, and uncertainty, they secured their position in the city of Badr in A.D. 627. In

 1843, a new sect—Babism—emerged. Its founder, Bab-ed-din, faced strong opposition from Persian clergy and government. He was arrested in 1850, hung by ropes against a wall of the city square in Tabriz, and shot to pieces by a regiment of one hundred soldiers. More than twenty thousand of his followers are believed to have lost their lives in the persecution which followed.

ONLY A YEAR AFTER THE CONCLUSION OF WORLD WAR II, international attention was focused on an unparalleled contest between the largest imperial power of the time—Great Britain—and an Indian freedom fighter whose philosophy of nonviolent action has had an incalculable influence throughout the world. Mohandas K. Gandhi first developed his technique of "satyragraha," or passive resistance, in South Africa to oppose racial discrimination. His principles of moral action against injustice and noncooperation with illegal authority evolved into the massive Indian freedom movement. Thousands of his followers courted voluntary arrest at the hands of the British, and Gandhi himself landed seven times in Indian jails before independence was achieved in 1947.

GANDHI, WHO ONCE ARGUED THAT "FREEDOM WON THROUGH bloodshed or fraud is no freedom," took his place in a long tradition of pacifists—most of whom were at some point in their careers imprisoned for their refusal to support war. The term "civil disobedience" itself originated with another "prisoner of conscience," Henry David Thoreau, who spent one night as a guest of the government in the Concord, Massachusetts, jail in July 1846. He had refused to pay a poll tax on the grounds that he could not support a government that endorsed slavery and was waging an imperialistic war against Mexico. He later justified his action in a lecture entitled "Civil Disobedience" and in which Thoreau claims that "under a government which imprisons any unjustly, the true place for a just man is also a prison."

LESS THAN A CENTURY LATER ANOTHER AMERICAN, EUGENE V. DEBS, became an inmate of Atlanta (Georgia) Penitentiary for opposing United States militarism—this time, involvement in World War I. Debs, who became known as Convict No. 9653, was indicted for a speech he made in Canton, Ohio, on a Sunday afternoon in 1918 where, as presidential candidate of the Socialist Party, he made plain his stand against the war. In the election of 1920, nearly a million Americans cast their votes for Convict No. 9653. The presidential winner, Warren G. Harding, commuted Debs's sentence a year later, but did not restore the citizenship of which he had been deprived.

WITH THE UNLEASHING OF NUCLEAR WEAPONRY IN 1945, PACIFISTS throughout the world found themselves facing an immense challenge. Among them was Bertrand Russell, founder of the campaign for nuclear disarmament and a philosopher whose work continues to have a profound influence on the course of modern philosophy. In 1954, he joined with Albert Einstein and other Nobel scientists in issuing a statement against nuclear proliferation and, in 1961, he led mass sit-downs in England for which the then-old man received a two-month prison sentence.

THE PERSECUTION, IMPRISONMENT, OR EXECUTION OF MANY OF THESE individuals would now constitute a violation of international human rights law. Ironically, the Dutch statesman and jurist Hugo Grotius, known as the father of international law, was himself just such a victim. In fact, he began work on one of his most celebrated legal treatises, *On the Law of War and Peace*, while serving a life sentence in the castle of Loevestein, after being convicted in 1618 for his role on the losing side of a religious and political controversy over the issue of free will and predestination.

IX

From those early beginnings, the idea of international law has steadily developed. Centuries later it saw the adoption of the Geneva Conventions, international treaties defining humanitarian law and protecting civilian populations and military personnel in time of war. But it was the end of World War II and the creation of the United Nations that put in place the whole contemporary framework for the development of international standards and mechanisms for the protection of human rights. What Antoine de Saint-Exupéry perhaps saw intuitively in the golden face of the peasant child sleeping on the night train was now codified in the Universal Declaration of Human Rights as "the inherent dignity" and the "equal and inalienable rights of all members of the human family." The declaration, adopted by a vote of the General Assembly of the United Nations on 10 December 1948, became the first globally applicable statement of the rights of all people.

The Universal Declaration of Human Rights has had an immense impact throughout the world. Many nations have enshrined its various articles in their constitutions and laws. To give legal form to the provisions of the declaration, the United Nations has adopted two international covenants that are legally binding upon every nation that becomes a party to them: the International Covenant on Economic, Social and Cultural Rights and the International Covenant on Civil and Political Rights. The two covenants, and an optional protocol, came into force in 1976; by the end of 1990, more than ninety nations had become parties to them. In this way, individual governments have volunteered to become accountable to an international body for protecting the human rights of their own citizens. This principle, of course, needs to be extended in practice until it embraces the entire world.

Those states that become voluntary parties to various human rights treaties may be required to submit reports on their practices; in some instances, they may become the object of international scrutiny by specially appointed United Nations *rapporteurs*; and, in Europe, all places of detention in a country are subject to on-the-spot inspection. But there exists no body that can require a government to change its laws and practices, no institution that can compel governments to respect the rights of their citizens. So there is still no gardener, no protector for human beings. The Mozart in everyone—child or adult—is still at risk. And, as the recent history of country after country has shown, the risk of murder at the hands of the state is very real indeed.

THE YOUNG PRISONER LIFTED THE TRAY OF FOOD THAT HAD BEEN PUSHED
into his cell. He felt something stuck to the bottom. It was a scrap of
paper. The handwritten note was badly smudged, but he could make out
the message on it: "We will never forget you. We will not rest until you
are free." It was a letter from Amnesty International. Suddenly he wept
uncontrollably, unable to halt the tears. He was one of thousands of
prisoners jailed without trial in a country under martial law. Word had
filtered into the prison that martial law was to be lifted, but he had heard no
other news. Nothing had changed for him. He wondered if he and other
prisoners had been forgotten. Then came the smuggled message. He had
not been forgotten.

FROM ANOTHER COUNTRY, AMNESTY INTERNATIONAL RECEIVED A
letter from a peasant leader. He too had been held without trial, kept
blindfolded without food or water. "We knew nothing about Amnesty
International before this," he wrote. "Until we were hunted, captured,
tortured, some murdered, and imprisoned, until all of our human rights
were violated. Apart from us, how many more have there been in my

country alone? How many more in the rest of the
world? Now we can understand the great task you
face. The fact that you who defend human rights
know of our detention gives us great hope.
Because of your intervention some people have
ceased to be persecuted, others were only half
tortured, others won their release from prison, and
others were not killed. All of this we owe to you."

DAY AFTER DAY AMNESTY INTERNATIONAL RECEIVES MESSAGES LIKE THAT,
full of hope and encouragement. But every day we get other urgent,
insistent messages. Appeals for help from prisoners, from their lawyers,
from their families and friends.

THE SEEDS OF AMNESTY INTERNATIONAL WERE PLANTED EARLY IN 1961
when a British lawyer named Peter Benenson read in his morning paper of
two students in Portugal who had been arrested in a restaurant and
sentenced to seven years' imprisonment for raising their glasses in a toast to
freedom. Indignant, Benenson's first reaction was to go to the Portuguese
Embassy in London and protest personally, but he realized that such an
individual gesture would accomplish little for the students themselves.
Government repression of dissent was a problem that had long troubled
him. During the 1950s he had attended political trials in Hungary, Cyprus,
South Africa, and Spain, either as a legal observer or as defense counsel. He
had also written and broadcast widely about the problem. Now he began to
wonder how oppressive regimes might react to concerted worldwide
protests against acts of political injustice. Gradually he conceived the idea of
a one-year international campaign to draw world attention to the plight of
people detained throughout the world—under all political systems—for the
peaceful expression of their political or religious opinions.

HE DISCUSSED THE IDEA WITH FRIENDS, AND THEIR ENTHUSIASTIC
reactions led him to write an appeal in *The Observer* newspaper, entitled
"The Forgotten Prisoners." The appeal, reported in the media in many
countries, announced the launching of a campaign called "Appeal for

Amnesty, 1961," whose object was to obtain an amnesty for all political and religious prisoners of conscience. Part of the campaign was the establishment of an office in London to collect information about such prisoners and to publicize individual cases.

THE APPEAL QUICKLY ATTRACTED INTERNATIONAL support and, within a few short months, the groundwork was laid for a permanent organization that eventually became known as Amnesty International. At the end of its first year, members were organizing national bodies in seven countries: Belgium, France, the Federal Republic of Germany, Ireland, the Netherlands, Sweden, and the United Kingdom. Based on small local groups bringing pressure to bear on behalf of victims held prisoner in other countries, the movement stressed the importance of political independence and strict impartiality. Within its first 12 months, the fledgling organization had sent four missions to make representations to the governments of Czechoslovakia, Ghana, the German Democratic Republic, and Portugal. Already there were 210 cases "under active investigation." A greeting-card campaign at the end of the year resulted in some 5,000 messages being sent to 12 prisoners in different countries.

THE ORIGINAL EMPHASIS ON BUILDING A MEMBERSHIP ORGANIZATION HAS remained central to Amnesty International's development. By working for individual victims in other countries, an international spirit has been kept alive, and the message that comes through is that human rights are not limited by national frontiers or by the boundaries of race and religion. The movement's activities focus strictly on prisoners, working to free all "prisoners of conscience"—people jailed solely for their beliefs or ethnic origins. It seeks fair and prompt trials for political prisoners and an end to torture and executions worldwide.

TODAY, 30 YEARS SINCE ITS INCEPTION, AMNESTY INTERNATIONAL HAS more than 1,100,000 members, subscribers, and regular donors in over 150 countries. They are to be found in Africa, Asia, the Americas, Australia, Eastern and Western Europe, and the Middle East. There are more than 4,200 local groups worldwide, with sections in 44 countries and territories. Since the four missions in its first year, Amnesty International has sent over 700 delegations to carry out on-the-spot investigation, observe trials, and meet government officials.

TO COUNTERACT VARYING PATTERNS OF POLITICAL REPRESSION, AMNESTY International uses a range of different techniques. A sustained campaign can be mounted on behalf of a long-term prisoner of conscience, but where prisoners are threatened with torture or death in custody, the first

response must be concentrated into the hours immediately after arrest. An "urgent action" network has been set up to guarantee rapid intervention when lives are feared to be at risk. This network is now able to count on volunteer coordinators in some sixty countries, ready to organize telegrams and express letters. They go into action virtually every day, and sometimes more than once a day, in dozens of countries every year. Hundreds of telegrams can be on their way within hours of receiving reports of possible torture. One government, replying to an Amnesty International appeal, said it had received ten thousand letters about a single case.

THE SCALE OF THE CHALLENGE IS VAST. PRISONERS OF CONSCIENCE ARE believed to be held in nearly half the countries in the world. In some fifty of them, political prisoners can be held without any charge or trial, often for months or even years. In the 1990s there is evidence of systematic torture being inflicted on prisoners in one of every three countries. The death penalty is in force in over one hundred countries and executions are often shrouded in secrecy. Censorship and intimidation make it impossible to construct a complete picture of these abuses. Some countries are virtually closed to the outside world. In many cases, there are simply no details available on individual prisoners' cases.

DOES IT WORK? OF THE MORE THAN 42,000 CASES TAKEN UP BY AMNESTY International since 1961, over 38,000 are now closed. Nonetheless, Amnesty International warns against measuring success by a "body count." If a measure is needed of the value of Amnesty International, it is the simple fact that people's inalienable rights continue to be abused. Every day it receives new calls for help, new messages from prisons, new testimony from victims. Encouragement comes from letters, not numbers. "I am free," wrote a prisoner from Benin on the day of his release. "I have just been freed this evening. I assure you that I owe my freedom to you. I survived thanks to you. It is true that one must never despair in life. This victory is completely yours, you who have been untiring workers. From this moment a new page of my life has been turned."

IT IS SOMETIMES CLAIMED THAT AMNESTY INTERNATIONAL—INDEED THE ideals for which it stands—is irrelevant or even antithetical to the interests of the nations of the Third World. There are other more immediate priorities, the argument runs, and bourgeois freedoms have never been part of those cultures. The growing international membership of Amnesty International belies this, with over half its sections in areas outside North America and Western Europe. Even more persuasive is the fact that those people who are struggling for human rights in their own countries throughout the world show with their actions that they do not consider the goal of freedom from arbitrary arrest, torture, and killing in any way foreign to their parts of the world or their own cultures.

AT THE XIDAN DEMOCRACY WALL IN BEIJING IN 1978, THOUSANDS OF Chinese citizens gathered to read the wall posters calling for democratic reforms in the country. On 29 November of that year, a "democracy symposium" was held in front of the wall. A Canadian journalist reported the words of one of the Chinese who spoke: "Never in our lifetime has there been a better chance to obtain the things we have dreamed of for so long. We are all fighting for a true democracy in our socialist motherland. It is unacceptable to the Chinese people that only the bourgeois West can enjoy the freedom of thought and action which is our right as human beings and as Chinese citizens. But this democracy will not be handed to us nor will it come just because we marched down a street and made speeches at Tienanmen. We are going to have to fight for it, and the struggle will be very hard and perhaps very long. But today, right now, we have a better chance than we ever had before. ...If we let this opportunity pass by, we will stand condemned by the suffering of the past and the expectations of the future."

SOMETIMES THE IMPACT OF AMNESTY International's work is brought home in the most graphic way possible, but in unexpected settings. In 1989, after a week of campaigning in Washington, D.C., the executive staff of the United States Section of Amnesty International were having dinner in a small restaurant. Though they were tired, the conversation never let up. It turned to the latest news of torture, killings, and "disappearances" in El Salvador. The waiter, who had appeared to pay no attention to the conversation, interrupted. Would it be possible for some of the kitchen staff to come over to the table? Three men came out of the kitchen. "Are you from Amnesty International?" asked one. "Sure. Where are you folks from?" came back the reply. "El Salvador. We heard you were here and we wanted to thank you." "Thank us for what?" "For saving our lives." The three grasped the hands of everyone at the table and wept. There was no other sound in the restaurant.

RELEASED PRISONERS OFTEN TALK OF THE IMPACT OF LETTERS FROM Amnesty International. "It is hard to describe the feelings in my heart," wrote one such former prisoner. "I regarded the letters as precious jewels." Another prisoner who had suffered two heart attacks under torture said he had lain near death in a hospital. "Someone smuggled a letter to me. It was a signal that the outside world was concerned. I decided to live another day. Then the officials themselves brought me the letters that had been arriving from all over the world. Before that I saw no point in living only to be tortured again and again. Now there was hope. I decided to live."

THE LETTERS OFTEN REACH THE HIGHEST LEVELS OF GOVERNMENT. Amnesty International delegations frequently report references by state officials to the flood of letters received by their governments. Amnesty International members are sometimes pleasantly surprised when they receive a signed reply to their appeals from a head of government.

THERE ARE OTHER WAYS IN WHICH TO EVALUATE THE CONTRIBUTION that Amnesty International has made. First, there has been progress in setting international standards for the protection of human rights. Amnesty International, together with other organizations, has pressed institutions like the United Nations to improve such standards. There is now a body of international law that establishes a common set of principles to protect citizens in all countries from abuses such as arbitrary arrest, torture, and summary execution.

SECOND, HUMAN RIGHTS HAS BEEN ESTABLISHED AS AN ISSUE transcending partisan politics, perhaps Amnesty International's most significant achievement. At a time when the human rights issue has been used as a propaganda weapon in both superpower and domestic politics, Amnesty International has often succeeded in lifting the question above the tangle of rhetoric and rivalries. When governments and opposition groups alike have been unable to divorce human rights from national political conflicts, Amnesty International has spoken for the rights of the victims, regardless of their political views.

THIRD, PUBLIC OPINION HAS BEEN MOBILIZED, PUTTING HUMAN RIGHTS firmly on the international agenda. The news media have taken up the issue, as have professional associations, other international bodies, and political leaders in various countries. Amnesty International continues to grow, attracting people who want to do something practical to help the victims.

OVER THE YEARS AMNESTY INTERNATIONAL HAS COMPILED A WEALTH OF detailed information on countries in all regions of the world. This ranges from information on laws, legal systems, and political structures to data on political arrests, torture, and execution. Collecting and verifying the information is a continuous process, undertaken by professional research staff at the organization's International Secretariat in London. Efforts are made to obtain information from a wide range of sources in order to build as complete a picture as possible and to distinguish between facts and allegations. New information comes from sifting the world press, government bulletins, and other public records. Other details come from interviews with witnesses, former prisoners, refugees, and prisoners' families and lawyers. Individual allegations are often extremely difficult to corroborate, and false stories may be given to the organization for a government's own purposes. Each piece of information is therefore carefully weighed and cross-checked to ensure accuracy. Government officials are questioned, often in the course of Amnesty International representatives' fact-finding missions to their countries. Frequently the research work does identify a consistent pattern of alleged violations, which is often supported by legal and/or medical evidence. The findings are then sent to the appropriate government for comment, with the assurance that any official reply will be made public.

OFTEN THE ACCOUNTS THAT AMNESTY INTERNATIONAL PUBLISHES MAKE sickening reading. Some people find them scarcely believable. It is worth recalling the words of the Mediterranean resistance fighters who wrote: "Sometimes, when we hear these reports about torture, we become frightened—as if the whole thing was unthinkable, as if we were the victims of a collective hallucination. But in actual fact, it is not the proof that is lacking, but the courage to believe the reports."

OF COURSE MUCH OF THE INFORMATION HAS ITS ROOTS IN THE PRISON cells and torture chambers; it finds its way to the outside world due to extraordinary feats of human ingenuity and courage. A former prisoner of

conscience told Amnesty International about his experience in custody. He was held in solitary confinement and given a very small amount of food. After his first few days in custody the prisoner in the next cell whispered to him through a gap in the wall. He said, "Good news. They are giving you food. That means they won't kill you. Maybe Amnesty International is working for you."

Sometime later the news went round the prison that he was about to be released. All night long, prisoner whispered to prisoner. Each one gave the next one the names of the prisoners in each cell. And all night long, the man who was about to be freed committed the names and personal details of each prisoner to memory. By dawn, the name of every prisoner in the entire prison had been whispered to him. Some had messages: "Contact my uncle." "Tell my mother I am still alive." He brought out from the prison the precious details of all those who remained behind in their cells.

REVULSION AT THE EXTERMINATION CAMPS OF WORLD WAR II LED TO A convention outlawing genocide for all time as a crime against humanity. Today's torture chambers demand a similar international response: the importance of an immediate international outcry wherever and whenever systematic torture and cruelty occurs cannot be overemphasized. A survivor of Auschwitz said that the victims suffered more profoundly from the indifference of the onlookers than from the brutality of the executioners. It was the silence of those he believed to be his friends, cruelty more cowardly, more subtle, that broke his heart. Increasingly the onlookers are refusing to remain silent.

WHAT SORT OF PEOPLE GET INVOLVED IN THE WORK OF AMNESTY International? They are people who hate injustice, who care about others, whose response to a news item on TV about people being tortured is to ask what they can do to help the victims.

THAT DESIRE TO DO SOMETHING PRACTICAL FOR THE VICTIMS IS probably the one thing that most Amnesty International members have in common. They come from dozens of countries and include carpenters and lawyers, students and firefighters, nurses and farmers, business executives and trade unionists. They are Buddhists, Christians, Jews, Muslims, atheists, and humanists. They are people who belong to all political parties and to no party at all.

AMNESTY INTERNATIONAL'S MONEY COMES FROM people's pockets. Individual members contribute annual fees; subscribers pay in subscriptions. Local groups' members organize street collections and fundraising events. And thousands of members of the public send in donations to keep the work going. Amnesty International has deliberately chosen to rely on this broad-based voluntary funding. This reflects the true character of the movement—its independence and impartiality—and maintains its basis in public support.

MUCH IS NOW KNOWN ABOUT THE DEGREE TO WHICH HUMAN RIGHTS are systematically abused. But is it impossible to say whether the world is now a better or worse place than it was thirty years ago. Many of the atrocities that Amnesty International opposes take place in secret. Sometimes information about torture and killing emerges long after the event. From some countries, almost no information about these problems comes to the outside world. What is clear is that the focus on human rights has sharpened. Many more people are coming forward with information. More journalists report on human rights questions. Governments are concerned about their international reputation. Bad publicity, diplomatic pressure, demonstrations, and international inquiries make a difference. The result: more information and more action.

IN TRYING TO ACHIEVE THE INTERNATIONAL PROTECTION OF HUMAN rights, Amnesty International has learned many lessons. No political system automatically protects human rights; therefore, vigilance must be worldwide. Exceptions must not be made: many governments argue that they are special cases, but human rights are universal and must be respected without exception. Accuracy and impartiality are of critical importance. Claims of human rights abuses are easily exaggerated and used for political ends; the truth must be established in every case regardless of political considerations.

BUT PERHAPS, ABOVE ALL, ONE FINAL LESSON HAS STOOD THE TEST OF time in almost every adversity. This lesson—for all those who are struggling to make a world respectful of the human rights of all—is very simply stated: Never give up. Some Amnesty International groups work on cases for years and years. Often they get no reply from the government and cannot make contact with the prisoner. But time and time again released prisoners tell of the impact of the constant campaign on their behalf, a campaign that many of them believe may have saved their lives.

A SCHOOL TEACHER WHO WAS A PRISONER OF CONSCIENCE FOR TEN years wrote to Amnesty International after his release: "I want you to know that from prison one can feel very much the support of friends (whom we do not know) who generously fight for our freedom. The task that you carried out for years is a hand stretched through the iron bars of prison, which in our worst moments makes us feel that we are never alone, that there is always hope and a feeling of love that has no frontiers and no languages, and which is present to tell us of the constant struggle of men and women of the world who want a more just humanity...."

Introductory text compiled by
RICHARD REOCH
International Secretariat, Amnesty International.

Recognition of the inherent dignity and of the equal and inalienable rights of all members of the human family is the foundation of freedom, justice and peace in the world,...

Excerpt from the Universal Declaration of Human Rights

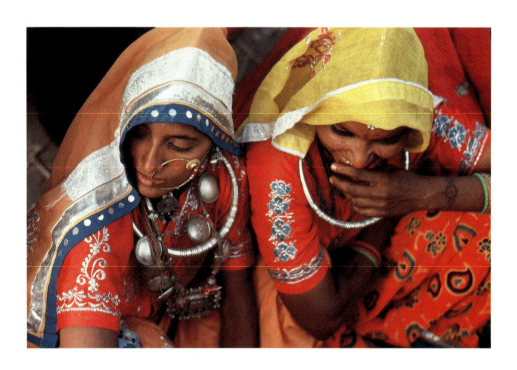

Pushkar fair, Rajasthan, India © RIC ERGENBRIGHT ▲

Tungsten mine near Bishop, California, U.S.A. © GALEN ROWELL/Mountain Light ▶

Violins will emerge from
   our tortured breasts,
The barbed wire will
   become violin strings,
The broken bones will
   become flutes,
There will be a wild dance.

MIKIS THEODORAKIS
*Greek composer, conductor, poet,
and political activist*

From *Journals of Resistance*. ©Flammarion 1971. English translation ©1973 by Hart-Davis MacGibbon Ltd. The lines are excerpted from "Our Sister Athina."

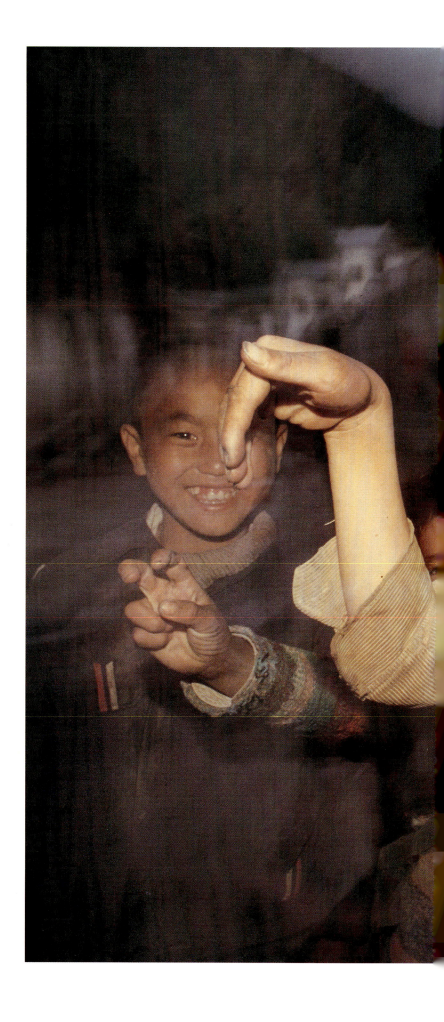

Tibet ©STEVE LEHMAN/Visions

Rama Cay, Nicaragua © WILLIAM F. GENTILE, from his book *Nicaragua*

It's really a wonder that I haven't dropped all my ideals, because they seem so absurd and impossible to carry out. Yet I keep them because in spite of everything I still believe that people are really good at heart. I simply can't build up my hopes on a foundation consisting of confusion, misery, and death. I see the world gradually being turned into a wilderness, I hear the ever approaching thunder, which will destroy us too, I can feel the sufferings of millions and yet, if I look up into the heavens, I think that it will all come right, that this cruelty too will end, and that peace and tranquillity will return again.

ANNE FRANK

From *The Diary of a Young Girl*

Falconer with goshawk, Khirgizia, U.S.S.R. ©FRANS LANTING/Minden Pictures

THE WAR GOD
(The Fall of France, 1940)

Why cannot the one good
Benevolent feasible
Final dove, descend?

And the wheat be divided?
And the soldiers sent home?
And the barriers torn down?
And the enemies forgiven?
And with no retribution?

Because the conqueror
Is the instrument of power
That hammers his heart
Out of fear of former fear.
When those he now vanquishes
Vanquished his hero-father
Surrounding his cradle
With fabled anguishes.

Today his victory
Chokes back fierce anxiety
Lest children of these slain
Prove dragon teeth sown,
Now their sun goes down,
Sprout tomorrow again
Stain the sky with blood
And avenge their dead fathers.

The killed, filled with lead,
On the helpless field
May dream pious reasons
Of mercy, but alas
They did what they did
In their own high season.

The world is the world
And not the slain
Nor the slayer forgive.
There's no heaven above
Ends passionate histories
In unending love.

Yet under wild seas
Of chafing despair
Love's need does not cease.

STEPHEN SPENDER
England

©1942 by Stephen Spender. Reprinted from *Selected Poems by Stephen Spender*. By permission of Faber and Faber LTD (UK) and Random House, Inc. (U.S.).

Imagine that you are confined within four walls, and that you have nothing left to eat or drink, and then a hand, unknown to you but generous, offers you a piece of bread and a glass of water.

Letter to Amnesty International from a former prisoner of conscience

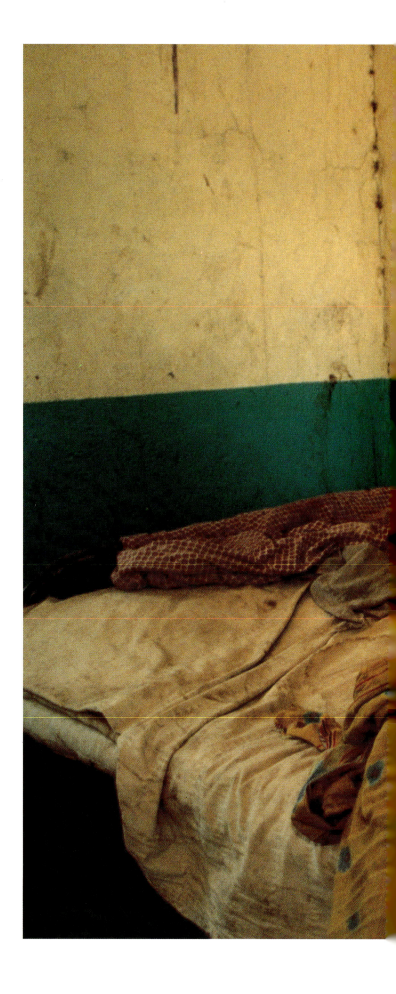

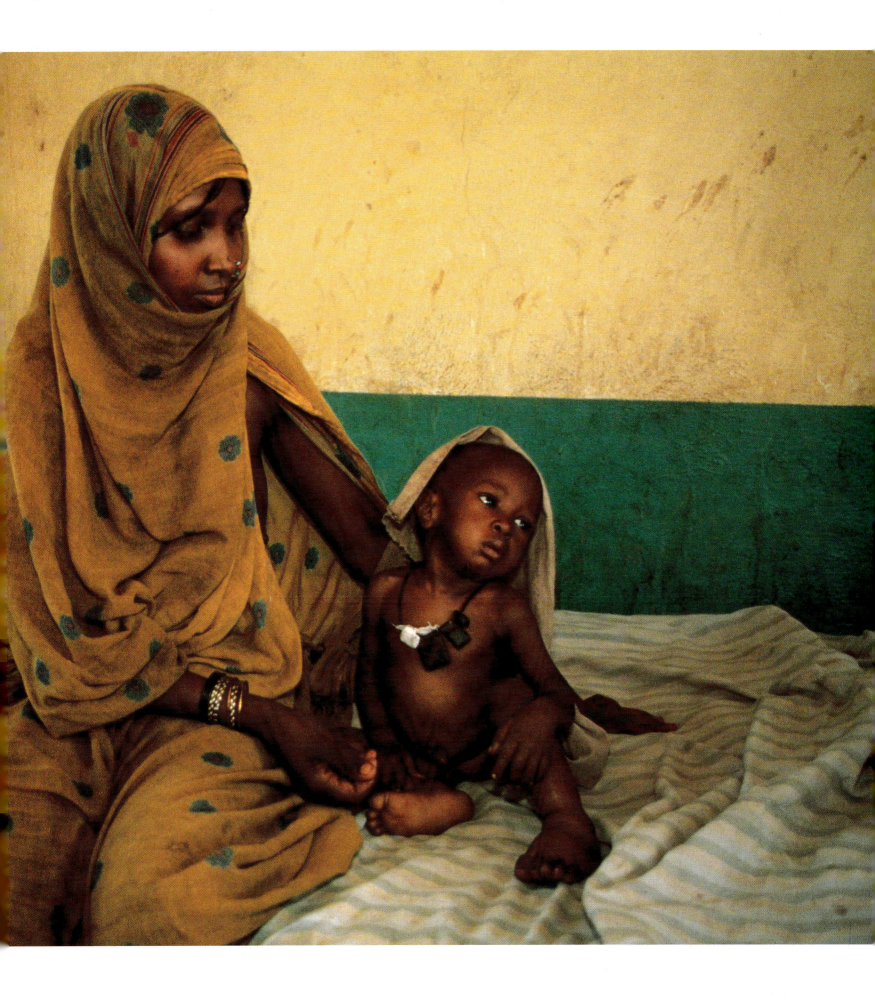

Kassala Refugee Camp, Sudan © CHRIS RAINIER

Sierra Leone ©MICHAEL KATAKIS/Visions

I am writing to inform you that after six years, four months, seventeen days in prison, I am free. I walked out of the prison gate with my shoulders unbent, my head unbowed. I can touch the green leaves of the trees. I can smell the sweet scent of flowers. I can share smiles and laughter with the women and children.

Surely there is nothing so sweet, so beautiful, so precious as freedom and liberty.

PROFESSOR MAINA WA KINYATTI
Former Prisoner of Conscience/Kenya

Poets always speak to someone.
With sword or wheat sheaf
They address the people
or sing softly
to a loved one,
revealing unexpected
dazzling scenes.
Their path is strewn with flowers.
But in my dark retreat
I bear poetry
like a secret disease,
a hidden
illicit fruit.

ALAIDE FOPPA
"Disappeared" poet and founder of the International Women's Association Against Repression/ Guatemala

Extract from "Words," translated by Rozenn Frere and Dennis Nurkse, in *You Can't Drown the Fire: Latin American Women Living in Exile* (Pittsburgh: Cleis Press, 1988). ©1988 Alicia Partnoy.

▲ *Girl from Ghashghaii tribe, Iran* ©JACQUES LOWE

◄ *Portugal* ©GEOFFREY CLIFFORD

Masai Mara National Reserve, Kenya © ALEX TEHRANI

No man is an island, entire of itself; every man is a piece of the continent, a part of the main;… Any man's death diminishes me, because I am involved in mankind, and therefore never send to know for whom the bell tolls; it tolls for thee.

JOHN DONNE
England

From "Meditation XVII" (1624) in *Devotions upon Emergent Occasions*.

I've always wished
you would see me
not by the exaggerations of the eye
but in the shape of God's creation
seen in the fulness of my being
because I stand complete on earth
like men in the whole universe.

SIPHO SEPAMLA
*Black author whose writings were
banned by the South African authorities*

Courtesy of Index on Censorship. ©1981.

Countryside near Seoul, South Korea ©ROBERT HOLMES

In spite of the tensions and uncertainties of our age, something profoundly meaningful has begun. Old systems of exploitation and oppression are passing away and new systems of justice and equality are being born. In a real sense ours is a great time in which to be alive.

MARTIN LUTHER KING, JR.
United States

Dairy farmers, Normandy, France ©DAVID W. HAMILTON/The Image Bank

NOTES FROM A POEM THAT CAN NEVER
BE WRITTEN

The facts of this world seen clearly
are seen through tears;
why tell me then
there is something wrong with my eyes?

To see clearly and without flinching,
without turning away,
this is agony, the eyes taped open
two inches from the sun.

What is it you see then?
Is it a bad dream, a hallucination?
Is it a vision?
What is it you hear?

The razor across the eyeball
is a detail from an old film.
It is also a truth.
Witness is what you must bear.

MARGARET ATWOOD
Canada

©1981 Margaret Atwood (Salamander Press).

Traditional Inca festival, Cuzco, Peru ©MICHAEL POWERS

Refugee camp, Afghanistan ©GEOFFREY CLIFFORD

Outside, the children play.
Inside, the silence and the dark.
Who will break the tunnel through
from one to the other?
Who will connect the two?

ANITA DESAI
India

Young tailors, Addis Ababa, Ethiopia ©JOHN ELK

The strongest motive for staying alive is that one has something for which one is determined to remain alive at all costs.

BRUNO BETTELHEIM
Survivor of the Dachau and Buchenwald concentration camps

From *The Informed Heart: Autonomy in a Mass Age* by Bruno Bettelheim. ©1960 by The Free Press, a division of Macmillan, Inc.; copyright renewed 1988 by Bruno Bettelheim. Reprinted by permission of the publisher.

Refugee camp, Baqa'a, Jordan © ROBERT AZZI/Woodfin Camp & Associates

You all are really wonderful people with such a kind golden heart. It is your untiring efforts that give helpless people a ray of hope, just like crystal-clear drops of water, so sweet and so refreshing for those journeying through unending deserts.

Former prisoner of conscience / Singapore

Letter to Amnesty International group member upon being released after more than 22 years in prison

If he were dead
I'd know it.
Don't ask me how.
I'd know.

I have no proof,
no clues, no answer,
nothing that proves
or disproves.
    There's the sky,
    the same blue
    it always was.
But that's no proof.
Atrocities go on
and the sky never changes.
    There are the children
    They're finished playing.
    Now they'll start to drink
    like a herd of wild
    horses.
    Tonight they'll be asleep
    as soon as their heads
    touch the pillow.
But who would accept that
as proof
that their father
is not dead?
The madness goes on
and children are always
    children.

ARIEL DORFMAN
Chilean exile, writer, and poet

Excerpt from the poem "Soft Evidence," from the book *Last Waltz in Santiago and Other Poems of Exile and Disappearance.* ©1988 Penguin Books. Reprinted by permission of the author.

Dumping ground for bodies, Haiti ©JIM TYNAN/Visions

Change and compel, slash us into shape,
But not our roots deep in the soil of old.
We are different hearts and minds
In a different body. Do not ask of us
To be deserters, to disown our mother,
To change the unchangeable.
The gum cannot be trained into an oak.

OODGEROO OF THE TRIBE NOONUCCAL
Australia

Extract from the poem "Assimilation—No!" in *My People* by Oodgeroo of the tribe Noonuccal (formerly Kath Walker), custodian of the land Minjerribah (Jacaranda Wiley Ltd.).

▲ *Hopi potter, Arizona, U.S.A.* © STEPHEN TRIMBLE

◄ *Shigatse trader, Tibet* © GALEN ROWELL/Mountain Light

Do not say that I'll
 depart tomorrow
because even today I
 still arrive…

I am the mayfly
metamorphosing on
 the surface of the
 river,
and I am the bird
 which, when spring
 comes,
arrives in time to eat
 the mayfly.

I am the frog swimming
 happily
in the clear water of a
 pond,
and I am also the grass-
 snake who,
approaching in silence,
 feeds itself on the
 frog…

My joy is like Spring,
 so warm it makes
 flowers bloom.
My pain is like a river
 of tears,
so full it fills up the four
 oceans.

Please call me by my
 true names,
so I can hear all my
 cries and my laughs
 at once,
so I can see that my joy
 and pain are but one.

Please call me by my
 true names,
so I can wake up,
and so the door of my
 heart can be left
 open,
the door of compassion.

THICH NHAT HANH
*Buddhist monk, teacher,
and peace activist exiled
from Vietnam since 1966*

Excerpt from "Please Call Me By My True Names" in *Being Peace* by Thich Nhat Hanh. Used by permission of Parallax Press. ©1987 Thich Nhat Hanh.

Novgorod, U.S.S.R. ©JIM BRANDENBURG

Young Balti women, Askole, Pakistan ©BARBARA CUSHMAN ROWELL/Mountain Light

Yesterday I saw you laugh
and the bars broke
the sun entered my eyes
and ran through all of me
spring wandered up the hall
breaking down doors
and because of your chuckles
the walls turned to dust
and the locks became bells
which sang
the birth of freedom
amongst the penitentiary ruins

VIVIANA HERRERA
Poet sentenced in 1983 to 19 years of imprisonment under the military government in Chile

Courtesy of Index on Censorship. ©1989.

Deep down we must have real affection for each other, a clear recognition of our shared human status. At the same time we must openly accept all ideologies and systems as means of solving humanity's problems. No matter how strong the wind of evil may blow, the flame of truth cannot be extinguished.

HIS HOLINESS
THE DALAI LAMA
OF TIBET,
TENZIN GYATSO

Petra, Jordan ©ROBERT HOLMES

I was so pleased with your letters.... they make me feel part of the human solidarity which grows in the world.... Day after day I believe the darkness in this world is going away.

Former prisoner of conscience/Jordan

Zambia © CAROL BERNSON/Visions

TO MY DAUGHTER:
A LETTER FROM PRISON

Listen:
My throat befriends the winds
to reach you, tender heart, fresh eyes.
Listen:
Hold a seashell up to your ear,
bring your ear close to this infamous earphone.
Listen:
The reason
is so simple and pure
as a drop of water
or a seed
that fits into the palm of your hand.
The reason is simple:
I just couldn't
stop fighting for the happiness
of those we call brothers and sisters.

ALICIA PARTNOY
Written in Villa Devoto Prison, Argentina

Translated by Sandra Wheaton. ©1978 Alicia Partnoy.

Village girls winnowing barley, Tarap Valley, Nepal © HUGH SWIFT

Bukavu, Eastern Zaire © ALEX TEHRANI

No dictatorship or authoritarian regime can now remain immune from the impact of world public opinion. There is no centre of power, be it in a democratic state or in a totalitarian regime, which can now ignore world public opinion for long.

SEAN MacBRIDE
Former political prisoner in Ireland; a founder of Amnesty International; only recipient of both the Nobel Peace Prize and the Lenin Peace Prize

Traditional Basque farming, Ceanuri, Spain ©GALEN ROWELL/Mountain Light

A POLITICAL PRISONER
LISTENING TO A CICADA

While the year sinks
    westward, I hear a
    cicada
Bid me to be resolute
    here in my cell,
Yet it needed the beat of
    those black wings
To break a white-haired
    prisoner's heart…
His flight is heavy
    through the fog,
His pure voice drowns
    in the windy world.
Who knows if he be
    singing still?
Who listens to me
    anymore?

LO PIN WANG
China

Where, after all, do universal human rights begin? In small places, close to home—so close and so small that they cannot be seen on any maps of the world. Such are the places where every man, woman and child seeks equal justice, equal opportunity, equal dignity, without discrimination. Unless these rights have meaning there, they have little meaning anywhere.

ELEANOR ROOSEVELT
United States
Former chairperson, United Nations Human Rights Commission

Extract from a 1948 speech.

Ambato market, Ecuador ©STEPHEN TRIMBLE

ADVICE TO THE OLD
(INCLUDING MYSELF)

Do not speak of yourself
 (for God's sake) even
 when asked.
Do not dwell on other
 times as different
 from the time
Whose air we breathe;
 or recall books with
 broken spines
Whose titles died with
 the old dreams. Do
 not resort to
An alphabet of gnarled
 pain, but speak of the
 lark's wing
Unbroken, still fluent as
 the tongue. Call out
 the names of stars
Until their metal clangs
 in the enormous
 dark. Yodel your way
Through fields where
 the dew weeps, but
 not you, not you.
Have no communion
 with despair; and, at
 the end,
Take the old fury in
 your empty arms,
 sever its veins,
And bear it fiercely,
 fiercely to the wild
 beast's lair.

KAY BOYLE
United States

From *This Is Not a Letter and Other Poems* (Sun & Moon Press). ©1985 Kay Boyle. Used by permission of the author.

Twin Minaret Mosque, Erzurum, Turkey © ROBERT MACKINLAY

To write to you
sun candy, my little girl,
I would…
I would have to gather so much tenderness…
And your mother, my love,
you mother is hard,
her soul is made of stone,
she hardly cries, ever…
except to write to you,
sun candy,
little moon crystal.

ALICIA PARTNOY
Written in Villa Devoto Prison, Argentina

Translated by Regina Kreger. ©1978 Alicia Partnoy.

Shona family, Eastern Highlands, Zimbabwe © ROBERT HOLMES ▲

Calbulco, near Puerto Montt, Chile © RIC ERGENBRIGHT ►

I stand here like a man
A man of immeasurable suffering, dead but obstinately upright.
Let me destroy this nightmare at last,
And realign the shadow of history.

I shall raise the children High, high, laughing for joy to the sun.

YANG LIAN
Exiled poet whose work was banned in China in the late 1980s

From Yang Lian's "Pagoda," from *Seeds of Fire: Chinese Voices of Conscience.* ©1988 by Geremie Barmé and John Minford. ©1986 by Far Eastern Economic Review Ltd. Reprinted by permission of Hill & Wang, a division of Farrar, Straus & Giroux, Inc.

Navajo man, Canyon de Chelly, Arizona, U.S.A. ©BARBARA BRUNDEGE/EUGENE FISHER

It is ten o'clock and the streets of the City are empty of people but flooded with fear. The invisible battle is being fought between the silent rage of the condemned and the arrogant leers of the Dictators. Somewhere a mother is losing all of her son save the torn piece of cloth she ripped from his shirt as the soldiers wrenched him from her embrace. He had been distributing pamphlets with the Truth written on them with the ink of the "disappeared." Now he too will join their invisible world, cease to officially exist.

We will pick up the pen that has fallen from his hand. Our care is as fundamental as the air we breathe, because we are writing for humans: your son, my brother, her mother. We are fighting for the humanity that flows out of all our fingertips. For the General cannot put the noose around the neck of freedom. It grows like a cathedral spire, rises like the birds up towards a brighter sun.

ANDREA PALFRAMAN
Eleventh-grade student, Canada

From *Writing for Rights: Poems and Stories for Amnesty International by Students in Canadian Schools*.

Vietnam ©GEOFFREY CLIFFORD, from *Vietnam: The Land We Never Knew* (Chronicle Books)

Nomadic Berbers, Middle Atlas Mountains, Morocco ©ROBERT HOLMES

Separation

If within my poems
You take out the flower
From the four seasons
One of my seasons
   will die
If you exclude love
Two of my seasons
   will die
If you exclude bread
Three of my seasons
   will die
And if you take away
   freedom
All four seasons and
   I will die.

SHERKO BEKAS
*Kurdish poet who spent
years of internal exile in
Southern Iraq*

Courtesy of Index on Censorship.
©1988.

Local photographer, Cuzco, Peru ©RIC ERGENBRIGHT

Evil acts swiftly, violently, and with a sudden crushing force. The good works more slowly, requiring time to reveal itself and bear witness. The good often arrives late. We are always on the lookout, always awaiting it.

RYSZARD KAPUSCINSKI
Poland

From *Warsaw Diary*. ©1985 Ryszard Kapuscinski. Reprinted by permission of Sterling Lord Literistic, Inc. First published in English in Granta 15, p. 221.

Egypt © GEOFFREY CLIFFORD

Whenever humanity seems condemned to heaviness, I think I should fly like Perseus into a different space. I don't mean escaping into dreams or into the irrational. I mean that I have to change my approach, look at the world from a different perspective, with a different logic and with fresh methods of cognition and verification. The images of lightness that I seek should not fade away like dreams dissolved by the realities of present and future…

ITALO CALVINO
Italy

Reprinted by permission of the publishers from *Six Memos for the Next Millennium* by Italo Calvino (Cambridge, Mass.: Harvard University Press). ©1988 by the Estate of Italo Calvino.

AMNESTY
INTERNATIONAL
AROUND
THE WORLD

AUSTRALIA: (Tel: 2 211 3566) Private Bag 23, Broadway, New South Wales 2007
AUSTRIA: (Tel: 222 505 4320) Wiedner Guërtel 12/7, A-1040 Wien
BARBADOS: (Tel: 809 424 4346) PO Box 872, Bridgetown
BELGIUM: Flemish (Tel: 3 271 1616) Kerkstraat 156, 2060 Antwerpen 6;
French (Tel: 2 538 8177) 9 rue Berckmans, 1060 Bruxelles
BERMUDA: (Tel: 809 29 27961) PO Box HM 2136, Hamilton HM JX
BRAZIL: (Tel: 11 813 5799) Rua Coropé 65, 05426 - São Paolo - SP
CANADA: English (Tel: 613 563 1891) 130 Slater St., Suite 900, Ottawa, Ontario K1P 6E2;
French (Tel: 514 288 1141) 3516 ave du Parc, Montréal, Québec H2X 2H7
CHILE: (Tel: 62 335 897) Señores, Casilla 4062, Santiago
CÔTE D'IVOIRE: (Tel: 324 660) 04 BP 895, Abidjan 04
DENMARK: (Tel: 33 11 75 41) Dyrkoeb 3, 1166 Copenhagen K
ECUADOR: (Tel: 2 503795) Señores, Casilla 240-C, Sucursal 15, Quito
FAROE ISLANDS: (Tel: 15816) PO Box 1075, FR-110 Torshavn
FINLAND: (Tel: 0 6931 488) Ruoholahdenkatu 24, SF-00180 Helsinki
FRANCE: (Tel: 1 43 38 74 74) 4 rue de la Pierre Levée, 75553 Paris (CEDEX 11)
GERMANY, FEDERAL REPUBLIC OF: (Tel: 228 650981-3) Heerstrasse 178, 5300 Bonn 1
GHANA: PO Box 1173, Koforidua, E.R.
GREECE: (Tel: 1 360 0628/363 1532) 30 Sina Street, 106 72 Athens
GUYANA: (Tel: 261 789) Palm Court Building, 35 Main Street, Georgetown
HONG KONG: (Tel: 300 1250/1251) Unit C, 3rd Floor, Best-O-Best Building,
32-36 Ferry Street, Kowloon
ICELAND: (Tel: 1 16940) PO Box 618, 121 Reykjavík
INDIA: (Tel: 11 310799) c/o Dateline Delhi, 21 North End Complex, Panchkuin Rd., New Delhi 110001
IRELAND: (Tel: 1 776361) Sean MacBride House, 8 Shaw Street, Dublin 2
ISRAEL: (Tel: 3 612 214) PO Box 23003, Tel Aviv 61230
ITALY: (Tel: 6 380 898/389 403) viale Mazzini 146, 00195 Rome
JAPAN: (Tel: 3 203 1050) Daisan-Sanbu Building 2F/3F, 2-3-22 Nishi-Waseda, Shinjuku-ku, Tokyo 169
LUXEMBOURG: (Tel: 48 16 87) Boîte Postale 1914, 1019 Luxembourg
MEXICO: (Tel: 5 658 9402 x303/304) Ap. Postal No. 20-217, San Angel, CP 01000 Mexico DF
NETHERLANDS: (Tel: 20 26 44 36) Keizersgracht 620, 1017 ER Amsterdam
NEW ZEALAND: (Tel: 4 849 774) PO Box 6647, Wellington 1
NIGERIA: PMB 59 Agodi, Ibadan, Oyo State
NORWAY: (Tel: 2 38 00 32) Maridalsveien 87, 0461 Oslo 4
PERU: (Tel: 14 466 772) Señores, Casilla 659, Lima 18
PORTUGAL: (Tel: 1 523 537) Apartado 1642, 1016 Lisboa Codex
PUERTO RICO: Calle El Roble No. 54, Altos, Rio Piedras
SENEGAL: Send all correspondence care of the International Secretariat, London
SIERRA LEONE: PMB 1021, Freetown
SPAIN: (Tel: 1 575 418) Paseo de Recoletos 18, Piso 6, 28001 Madrid
SWEDEN: (Tel: 8 663 1900) Gyllenstiernsgatan 18, S-115 26 Stockholm
SWITZERLAND: (Tel: 31 25 79 66) PO Box 1051, CH-3001 Bern
TANZANIA: PO Box 4331, Dar es Salaam
TUNISIA: (Tel: 1 35 34 17) 48 Avenue Farbat Hached, 3e Etage, 1001 Tunis
UNITED KINGDOM: (Tel: 71 278 6000) 99-119 Rosebery Avenue, London EC1R 4RE
USA: (Tel: 212 807 8400) 322 8th Avenue, New York, NY 10001
URUGUAY: (Tel: 2 91 5841) Yi 1333 Apto. 305, Montevideo
VENEZUELA: (Tel: 2 575 3279) Apartado 5110, Carmelitas 1010-A, Caracas

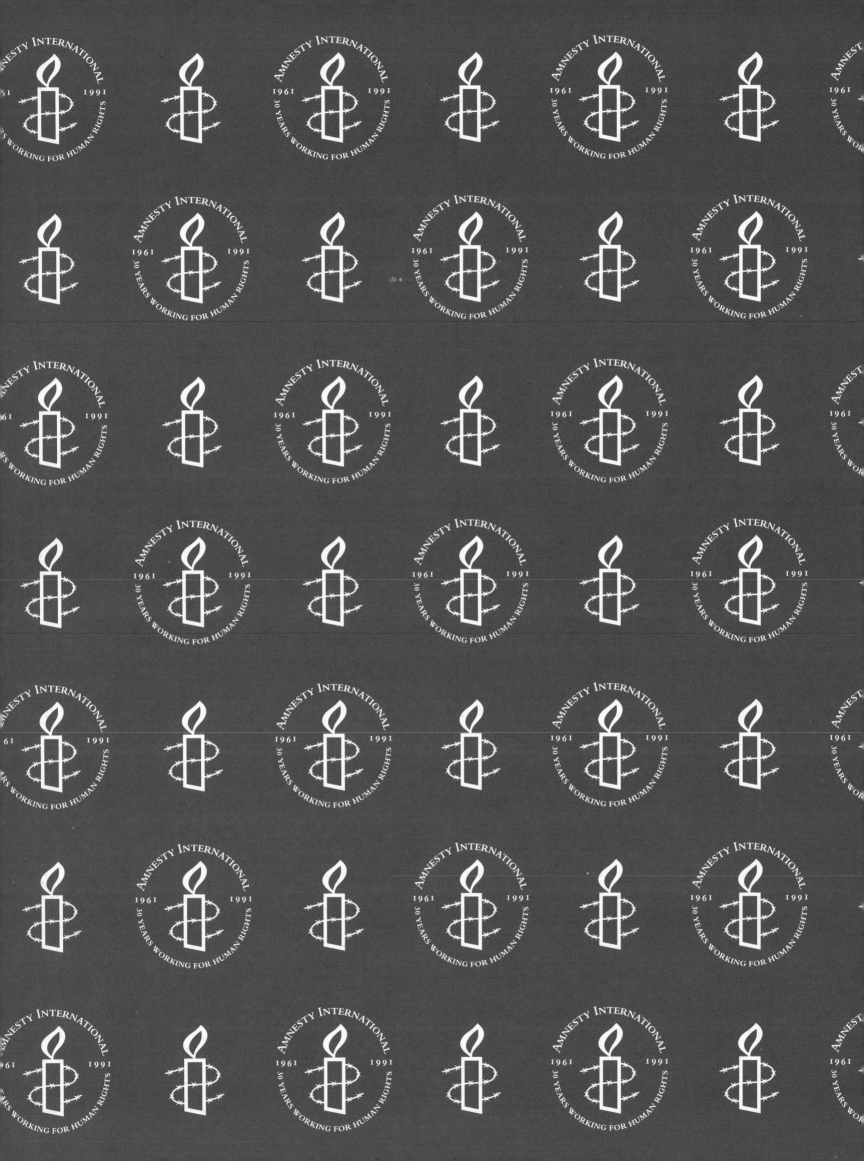